JOHN WY

MESOLITHIC BRITAIN

SHIRE ARCHAEOLOGY

2

Cover illustration
Reconstructed mesolithic hunting scene.
(Illustration: Tim Taylor.)

British Library Cataloguing in Publication Data:
Wymer, John.
Mesolithic Britain. — (Shire archaeology).
1. Great Britain. Palaeolithic civilization
and Mesolithic civilization. Archaeological source.
I. Title.
936.101.
ISBN 0-7478-0121-5.

Published by
SHIRE PUBLICATIONS LTD
Cromwell House, Church Street, Princes Risborough,
Buckinghamshire HP17 9AJ, UK.

Series Editor: James Dyer.

Copyright © John Wymer, 1991.
All rights reserved.
No part of this publication may be reproduced or transmitted
in any form or by any means, electronic or mechanical,
including photocopy, recording, or any information storage
and retrieval system, without permission in writing
from the publishers.

ISBN 0 7478 0121 5

First published 1991.

Printed in Great Britain by
C. I. Thomas & Sons (Haverfordwest) Ltd,
Press Buildings, Merlins Bridge, Haverfordwest, Dyfed SA61 1XF.

Contents

Acknowledgements

I wish to express my thanks to all my colleagues and the museums for supplying the photographs, as named in the captions.

List of illustrations

1
Introduction

The term *mesolithic* was used in the late nineteenth century to describe the period between the old and the new stone ages. These were already clearly defined and graced by classical language as the *palaeolithic* and *neolithic* periods. The palaeolithic period was represented by flint tools and some rare human fossils ranging over an ill defined but great length of time, when hunting and foraging were the only methods of subsistence. The neolithic period, in contrast, although devoid of metals, contained evidence of simple farming economies. Already it was obvious that the latter part of the palaeolithic, referred to as the 'cave' period as opposed to the earlier 'drift' period, was considerably advanced: the people were of modern type (that is, our own species, *Homo sapiens sapiens*), with a greatly expanded kit of flint and bone tools and weapons, evidence of artistic expression and semi-permanent settlements. Yet even this degree of development was seemingly far removed from the earliest agricultural societies, recognised as probably originating in the Near East and gradually spreading across Europe, to reach Britain and Scandinavia almost last of all. There must have been something in between, something in the middle, hence the adoption of the term *mesolithic* or *middle stone age*. It was an unfortunate choice, for in a continuum there is no middle, no hard line between the form of one society and another, or necessarily any contemporaneity which is implied. However, the term has stuck and, even if it means something entirely different in Africa, its meaning in Britain is quite clear: it means all the evidence for human activity in Britain since the final disappearance of glacial ice in Scotland (taken for convenience at 8300 bc, but see below for comment on dates given in calendar years) and the establishment of farming economies in the fourth millennium bc.

The discarded flint tools and weapons of the mesolithic period were often found by flint collectors in the latter part of the nineteenth century. Particularly distinctive were the microliths: very small flint blades delicately chipped into points of various forms. They were called 'pygmy flints' and usually regarded as neolithic.

Who were these mesolithic people? Where had they come

from, or were they already in Britain? Why did they not
domesticate animals and sow grain as was done in the Near
East from the eighth millennium BC? What kind of life did
they lead? How do we know that they were in Britain at
all? Archaeologists can answer some of these questions. This
book describes the type of evidence that is available and
some of the current ideas on what it is thought it means.

Comparison has often been made between the apparently
simple life of mesolithic hunter-gatherers and the superior
progressive achievements of their contemporaries in south-
west Asia but, as Professor J. G. D. Clark has emphasised,
the potential for change would have been just the same.
Factors of circumstance and environment dictated the manner
in which mesolithic people adapted themselves to their
surroundings. The most significant aspect of the mesolithic
period in Britain, and elsewhere in much of Europe, is the
manner in which these descendants of Upper Palaeolithic
populations reacted to a whole range and sequence of
ecological changes. At first they wrested a living from an
open, almost treeless landscape, but they had to adapt to
coniferous and then deciduous forest. This changing scene,
resulting from the gradual amelioration of the climate from late
glacial to interglacial conditions, was probably too slow to be
noticed in one generation, but knowledge of it may have persisted
in folklore of some kind.

There is growing evidence that earlier hunters, who were
mainly dependent on large herds of animals such as reindeer,
were restricted to the open landscapes in which such herds
were to be found. It has been suggested that one of the
main reasons for the breakdown of the once highly successful
hunting communities of the Upper Palaeolithic was the
gradual afforestation of the post-glacial landscape. The mesolithic
people adapted in many different ways: hunting forest animals
such as roe and red deer, using marine resources, fishing
and wildfowling. The hafted flint axe is a symbol of their
ingenuity. It may be an exaggeration to credit them with its

1. Microliths found at Hastings, East Sussex, in the nineteenth
century and referred to as 'pygmy flints'. Actual size.

invention, but they made and used these axes to an extent that had not been seen before in the Old World. In this sense they were acting in a similar manner to their Near Eastern counterparts, for they were adapting the environment to themselves and not the reverse, as had been the lot of humanity for well over a million years! Scrubland on the poor light soils of such areas as the Pennine moors, the sandy areas of the Weald and perhaps the Brecklands of East Anglia was burnt off, seemingly deliberately, in order to keep the land open and to encourage the growth of young shoots and, in turn, the grazing animals which the people could cull. Timber was used for boats, bows, spears, tent-frames and a host of other things that have perished. Little remains of perishable artefacts on the known mesolithic sites of Britain, although much must exist under wetlands such as the Fens, but some of the continental and Irish material is described and illustrated in this book to fill some of the gaps.

Radiocarbon dating

The dates used in this book are given in radiocarbon years (bc) with the standard deviation expressed as plus or minus a particular number of years. It must be realised that radiocarbon years are known to be younger than actual calendar years (BC). This has been determined by the checking of radiocarbon measurements against ancient fossil trees where tree-ring analysis (dendrochronology) can give the precise date in calendar years of the piece sampled. The calibration of the two is not straight-forward as the variations are irregular, so no attempt is made to do so here. However, as a rule of thumb, a radiocarbon date of 6000 bc may be nearly a thousand years too young and 4000 bc perhaps about 4700 BC. Radiocarbon dates can also be expressed as bp or BP, that is before the present in radiocarbon years or in calendar years respectively. All the dates are calculated as before 1950 and not the year in which the sample was measured. Yet another point to consider is that the date is really an expression of probability. A standard deviation (SD) is always given with the date in the form of plus or minus so many years. This means that the actual radiocarbon date probably lies some-where within the span of time represented by the addition and subtraction of the SD to the date quoted. For example, a date quoted as 7000 ± 100 bc has a probability of being somewhere between 6900 and 7100 bc. With one SD the probability is 66 per cent likely that the date lies within this range; with two SDs the probability is 95 per cent likely that the date would be between 6800 and 7200 bc. In neither case does it mean that it is more likely to be at one end or in the middle of the range. Obviously, the more radiocarbon measurements made at one site and shown as bars indicating the time range instead of specific dates, the more reliable will be the data. In spite of these considerations, it is still the most useful way of assessing both the relative and the chronometric ages of mesolithic sites.

2
At the end of the last ice age

About 18,000 years ago an ice sheet covered much of Britain. Most of southern Britain was free of actual ice, but it would have been an inhospitable open landscape, subject to permafrost and chilling winds. Mammoths and other animals adapted to such conditions probably found enough to eat and during the short summers it may have been possible for groups of human hunters to roam across the area in search of prey, even in sight of the ice sheet. Reindeer may have attracted them. However, no people could exist where the land was buried beneath great thicknesses of ice, which included nearly all of Wales and Ireland. The Midlands remained free but ice covered much of what is now the North Sea and fringed the east coast as far south as north Norfolk.

Gradually the ice sheets receded as the climate slowly warmed — a global change but affected by such local factors in Britain as topography and the position of the Gulf Stream. This Late Glacial period, as it is called, was a complex one, for there appears to have been a relatively rapid rise in the annual temperature about 11,500 bc, only to be followed by another slow cooling of the climate. This culminated in a re-advance of glaciers into Scotland (the Loch Lomond Stadial) and it was not until about 8300 bc that the temperature rose once again and Britain became free of ice for the last time. This is the accepted date for the beginning of the mesolithic period, but it is merely a date of archaeological convenience. As will be seen in the next chapter, it does not imply the reoccupation of an uninhabited region.

The study of insect remains has shown that the climate ameliorated at the end of the Late Glacial far more quickly than might be deduced from the contemporary vegetation. The latter can be revealed by the analysis of fossil pollen in sediments, but allowance has to be made for the re-colonisation of the barren post-glacial landscape; seeds had to travel and soils had to develop which suited their germination. Tree species are especially important for giving an accurate picture of the environment, both by the species represented and by the proportion of tree pollen to that from the flora generally associated with an open landscape. It is thus possible to visualise the scenery encountered by mesolithic people at dif-

Years bc	Chronozones	Pollen zones and climatic periods	Events	Position of key sites as indicated by radiocarbon dates
3000				Wawcott
				Oronsay shell middens
				Eskmeals
4000	Early-temperate	VII Atlantic (warm and wet)	Lower peat of East Anglian fens	Low Clone
5000				Culver Well
				Cherhill
				Shippea Hill
			English	Westward Ho!
6000		VI Late Boreal (warm and dry)	channel breached	
				Filpoke Beacon
7000	Pre-temperate	V Early Boreal (increasing warmth)	Rise in sea level	Oakhanger 'Cheddar Man' and Aveline's Hole cemetery
8000		IV Pre-boreal	Sea line beyond Dogger Bank	Star Carr Thatcham
	Loch Lomond Stadial	III Younger Dryas (cold)	Last ice in Scotland	
9000		II Allerød (warmer)		Sproughton barbed points
10000	Windermere Interstadial			
		I Older Dryas (cold)		Gough's Cave Robin Hood's Cave Creswell Poulton-le-Fylde barbed points
11000	Dimlington Stadial			
12000				

FLANDRIAN STAGE

DEVENSIAN STAGE — LATE GLACIAL

2. Chronology of the Late Glacial and mesolithic period.

ferent times during the five thousand years they were present. There were great changes during this time. Figure 2 shows the chronology that has been established, mainly by a combination of pollen analysis and radiocarbon dating. There was an open steppe-like landscape in the wake of the Late Glacial with

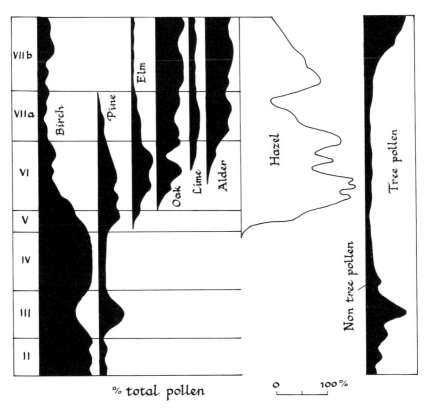

% **total pollen**   0   100%

3. A simplified pollen diagram from a dried-up lake at Hockham Mere, Norfolk. The level thought to be contemporary with nearby mesolithic occupation shows some deforestation and, among the herb pollen, a rise in ivy (*Hedera*). This may have been brought in by the people to feed or attract deer. Such pollen analysis gives an accurate record of the local vegetation through time and the tree pollen clearly indicates the gradual change from a birch/pine forest to the deciduous woodland of the later Atlantic period (zones VIIa-b). Note the high frequency of hazel (*Corylus*) from zone V. The curve for hazel is usually left open in pollen diagrams as it is classified as a shrub rather than a tree. Although the same general sequence can be found over most of Britain, similar pollen diagrams from different sites do not necessarily imply that they are contemporary, for many factors have to be considered, such as geographical situation, local climate, types of soil, the activity of grazing animals and also the interference of human groups.

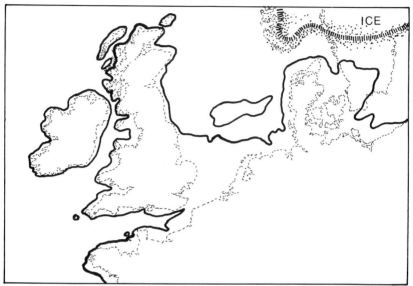

4. The geography of north-west Europe at the beginning of the mesolithic period, about 8000 bc. The approximate position of the coastline at that time is shown by a thick black line. Glacial ice had left Scotland but still remained over much of Scandinavia.

birch trees and some pine (Pre-boreal). Gradually the pine dominated and much of Britain would have resembled the coniferous forests found in northern Scandinavia today (Boreal). The climate was drier than now and a little cooler, but it slowly became warmer and wetter (Atlantic). Deciduous trees such as oak, alder and elm established themselves and a dense forest covered much of Britain. Figure 2 also gives the radiocarbon dates of some important mesolithic and earlier sites, as well as some climatic and geographical events.

A typical pollen diagram is shown in simplified form (figure 3). It is from the sediments of a dried-up lake in Norfolk and records a long history of vegetational and climatic change, much of which spans the mesolithic period.

The subsistence and lifestyle of the mesolithic people in Britain have to be assessed against this changing background. Equally important were the dramatic geographical changes that happened during the same period in response to the worldwide rise in sea-level as the great polar ice caps shrank, so returning water to the oceans. At the end of the Late Glacial a land bridge existed between eastern Britain, Denmark and the Low Countries, now 30 metres or more beneath the waters of the North Sea. The great European rivers such as the Rhine and Thames probably flowed through what is now the Straits of Dover. Figure 4 shows the geography of this time and, although marshy places, lakes and other obstructions must have existed, movement was certainly possible from what is now the European mainland to Britain. Britain was thus just the most north-westerly tip of a peninsula linked to the great plains of central and eastern Europe. Apart from being a corridor, this lost land beneath the North Sea was probably a much favoured area for the early mesolithic people. A fine barbed point of antler was dredged up in the net of a trawler within a block of 'moorlog' (the peat which formed on this old land surface) on the Leman and Ower Banks, 40 km off the Norfolk coast at a depth of 39 metres. Many unreachable mesolithic sites must lie beneath the North Sea.

Rising of the land as a result of the removal of the enormous weight of ice after the Late Glacial complicates the effect of rising sea-levels, and in parts of Scotland the land surfaces of this time are now above the sea-level instead of under it. In southern Britain the rise was continuous in relation to the land. River valleys which had drained over this submerged land silted up in their estuaries, creating buried channels. The Fens of East Anglia began to form as the drainage was impounded. Eventually the sea rose to a height whereby it flowed into the south-westward flowing major rivers, the Straits of Dover were breached and the North Sea and the Atlantic were linked. Britain was now an island. This breaching of the English Channel at some time around 6500 bc makes a convenient division between the earlier and later mesolithic periods in Britain.

5. Barbed point of red-deer antler trawled from the Leman and Ower Banks in the North Sea, about 40 km north-east of Cromer. It is 22 cm long. (Photograph: Castle Museum, Norwich. Copyright: Norfolk Museums Service.)

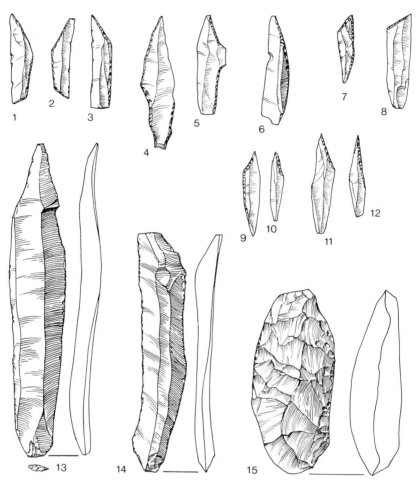

6. Late Glacial and earlier mesolithic flintwork. The occurrence of distinctive assemblages of types of flint tools and weapons (referred to as industries by archaeologists when they occur repeatedly at different sites) suggests that during this period various groups of people with their own traditions were occupying or travelling around and between Britain and north-west Europe. Late Glacial: (Creswellian points) 1, Aveline's Hole; 2, Gough's Cave; 3, Robin Hood's Cave, Creswell Crags; (tanged point) 4, Hengistbury Head; (shouldered point) 5, Hengistbury Head; (penknife point) 6, Crown Acres, Newbury. Late Glacial or earlier mesolithic: (Creswellian-like points) 7, Titchwell; 8, Hockwold; (long blades) 13-14, Titchwell. Earlier mesolithic: (microliths) 9-10, Star Carr; 11-12 Thatcham; (axe) 15, Broxbourne. The earlier mesolithic industry, comparable to the Danish 'Maglemosian', may have originated in the area now covered by the North Sea. At first it was probably contemporary with other industries surviving from the Late Glacial but by the end of the eighth millennium it was the only one present in Britain. All half size.

3
Natives and newcomers

There is plenty of evidence to show that groups of hunter-gatherers occupied Britain at various times during the Late Glacial period (11,500-8300 bc), but it is difficult to know whether these were indigenous people with territories restricted to the present geographical boundaries, or whether they may have been roaming parties with a territory that extended across to the plains of northern and eastern Europe, in view of the lack of any sea barrier. At the end of the Late Glacial, ice still covered most of Scandinavia as far south as the present Baltic, which was then a much larger inland sea. Both possibilities may be true and the shores of the Baltic, the land now under the North Sea, the river valleys and lakes of southern and eastern Britain and the natural caves and rock shelters of the Mendips and Peak District in particular may have been the hunting grounds of numerous small groups. Some of these groups may have followed traditional seasonal routes; others may have used base camps within defined territories. Certainly, there are similarities between some of these Late Glacial flint industries of north-west Europe and those found in Britain. There are also differences, but what these variations imply is difficult to assess. All of these people shared an inherited tradition of working flint in a manner that can be traced throughout the whole of the Upper Palaeolithic period in Europe, starting at about 40,000 years ago. The basic technology remained the same, but certain features and innovations warrant the names archaeologists give to those that are especially distinctive. It seems most likely that such distinctions do represent different groups of people but with a common 'cultural' connection. At the beginning of the mesolithic period in Britain there may have been at least three such groups exploiting the area:

1. A group making a large proportion of very long, elegant flint blades apart from the usual repertoire of scrapers, burins and other tools. Microliths are rare; there are a few small blades truncated obliquely and no axes.
2. Another group with an emphasis on shouldered and tanged points.
3. A further group with large numbers of simple oblique or triangular microliths and usually with flint axes.

Some typical examples of these three distinctive early mesolithic flint industries are shown in figure 6. The first 'long-blade group' would seem to have its origins in the Creswellian of the Late Glacial period, so well represented in the Cheddar caves, Somerset, and at Creswell Crags, Derbyshire, dating around 10,500 bc, although similar Creswellian sites are found in the Low Countries. There may also have been influences from northern France, where somewhat similar 'long-blade industries' occur in the very early post-glacial period. None of the British sites is yet securely dated, but they appear to span the period from the end of the Late Glacial into the early mesolithic. They occur invariably along river valleys and there is an important site at Sproughton near Ipswich, Suffolk, where there was an outcrop of fine-quality flint which was skilfully knapped into long and shorter blades. This was beside the river Gipping and may be of Zone IV Pre-boreal date (see figure 2). At this point the river Gipping had filled a buried channel with gravel and sand during the end of the Late Glacial and a few similar blades and cores have come from this gravel, so it would seem that people with the same style of flintworking had been living in or at least visiting the area over a long period. Also in this gravel were two broken barbed points of antler and bone. Such weapons are further considered below. Other long-blade sites occur along the valleys of the Little Ouse and Wissey in East Anglia, around the edge of the Fenland, and just below sea-level off the north Norfolk coast near Brancaster. They have been found in the lower Thames valley near Northfleet, Kent, higher up the valley at Goring, Oxfordshire, and along its tributaries: the Colne at Uxbridge, Middlesex, along the Kennet valley and at several other sites. Some of the larger blades show a crushed or 'mashed' edge, which can be replicated by the heavy use of such blades in a chopping action against hard wood, bone or antler, so some specialised activity could account for their production, and the proximity to rivers may not be coincidental.

Flint industries with shouldered and tanged points are not commonly found. The best known is that from Hengistbury Head, Dorset, but this is not truly mesolithic as it dates to the Late Glacial. It has been compared to the reindeer-hunting camps around north-west Germany, particularly at Ahrensburg, where similar shouldered or tanged points were found, also of Late Glacial age. Isolated undatable finds of such points are occasionally made, but it cannot be reliably assessed whether the groups responsible for them were much of an influence on the early mesolithic of Britain. However, in the same region of

7. Submerged Boreal forest exposed at low tide, Titchwell, Norfolk. Beneath occurred the flints of a long-blade industry on an old land surface. (Photograph: D. Wicks, Norfolk Archaeological Unit.)

Germany there are industries with so-called 'penknife points' and these occasionally turn up in Britain in apparently early mesolithic contexts.

It is the third group that is our main concern, for it does not occur until after the end of the Late Glacial and is the dominant industry of the whole early mesolithic. At Star Carr, North Yorkshire, and Thatcham, Berkshire, it is dated by radiocarbon and pollen to the Pre-boreal and Boreal zones. During the eighth millennium the distribution of the distinctive flint industry shows that these people spread into most of England, as far as the West Country and on to the Yorkshire Moors, and to South Wales. By 7000 bc or not long after, parts of Scotland and Ireland began to be occupied.

It is not known how long some of the earlier 'Creswellian' traditions may have persisted but, if the association of the bones and flintwork at Anston Cave in Derbyshire is reliable, the radiocarbon dates would suggest that reindeer were still being hunted by people with such traditions as late as about 7900 bc. This would imply that a more open environment existed in this

part of the north Midlands, contemporary with developing coniferous forest in the south to which other groups were adapting.

The earlier mesolithic flintwork in Britain is often referred to
as a 'broad-blade industry', in order to differentiate it from the
later mesolithic industries with numerous small narrow blades
which were required as blanks for the particular types of microliths then in vogue.

During this period the sea-level was encroaching upon much
of the land between Britain and the continent, although it is
unlikely that communication was very difficult. Rafts or boats
would certainly have been necessary to reach Ireland. The
British coastline was still, in most places, some distance from its
present one, so it is not surprising that, although almost every
other type of environment was being exploited, there is no
evidence for the use of marine resources. Such sites presumably
existed but have long since been submerged. At the beginning of
the post-glacial, almost identical flint industries are found in
Jutland known as Maglemosian, so this suggests that the area in
between was also occupied. However, by the end of the eighth
millennium marked differences begin to appear between the
British and Danish sites, particularly in the design of their
barbed points of antler and bone, so it would seem that contacts
were ceasing. At the same time, there is some indication that
other mesolithic groups, with their origins in central and southern
France, made their way into Britain. They brought with them a
tradition of different forms of microliths, often geometric in
shape.

The use of bone and antler for the production of various tools
and weapons has already been mentioned in regard to barbed
points. They had a long ancestry, dating back to the classical
Magdalenian of the French later Upper Palaeolithic, the period
associated with so much of the magnificent cave art in southern
France and northern Spain. Hundreds of such weapons were
found in the reindeer camps of the Late Glacial in north-west
Germany, and a number have been found in Britain in both
Late Glacial and early mesolithic contexts. The richest site in
Britain for barbed points is Star Carr, where nearly two hundred
were found. Others come from several sites in Yorkshire, one
from Royston, Hertfordshire, and two broken ones were dredged
out of the river Thames at Battersea and Wandsworth in London.
All these would appear to date to the early mesolithic, before
about 7000 bc. Their distribution on the eastern side of England
is very marked.

The period from 8000-7000 bc saw immense changes in the climate and landscape. At the beginning there was a relatively bare open landscape, and at the end thick coniferous forest. The effect upon the mammals on which the mesolithic people depended for their subsistence was considerable. The reindeer had already disappeared and as the forest grew so the horse had to find pastures elsewhere. Red and roe deer flourished in the forest, as did wild boar. The elk died out. The smaller mammals such as beaver and pine marten adapted to the new landscape, as did wolves and foxes. Aurochs survived, but probably in reduced numbers.

Thus by the time Britain became an island all but the more inhospitable places, such as in the Highland zones, were exploited by people whose movements were more restricted than those of their ancestors. It would have been a small population, for hunter-gatherers need large territories to survive comfortably. It is likely that by the later mesolithic groups had their own defined territories in order to prevent conflict. There is no convincing evidence that newcomers arrived in any numbers, if at all, during this time, and an insular British mesolithic developed, totally unaware of the momentous events in the Near and Middle East, where the cultivation of crops, the domestication of animals and urbanism were leading to literate civilisation, the repercussions of which would bring their world to an end, but that would not be for nearly another three thousand years.

8. Map showing some Late Glacial and earlier mesolithic sites, mostly referred to in the text.

4
Subsistence

The procurement of food is the obvious first essential activity of any society. Those who live solely by hunting and foraging must organise their existence with great care if they are not to be ever on the move, with each day a precarious gamble for survival. All the evidence suggests that life during the mesolithic period was anything but such an existence. Occasional disasters, tragedies or lean times there must have been, as in any economy, but sites or areas were chosen with forethought, based on the inherited experience of countless generations. These people would have possessed a vast knowledge of plants, edible or otherwise, and of animal behaviour. The success of their economy was due to their apparent exploitation of a great variety of resources, thus avoiding the danger of becoming dependent on one or just a few food items. The archaeological record is hazy, but the way of life most likely to fit the evidence is the establishment of base camps from which hunting and foraging parties would operate. This implies the selection of sites for the resources known to be available within daily reach. This could mean within a radius of about 10 km, or about two hours' walking, depending on the geography of the area. Such could hardly support more than three or four small family units, so groups of about ten or twenty people at the most can be postulated. The selection of a base camp would, however, not restrict hunting and foraging to the immediate area and hunters especially would often go off on forays for one or more nights, making temporary camps, probably in places used regularly. Long use of a base camp would produce a sense of territory but there is no reason to suppose that, with the small population and the area of land available, this would cause conflict with other groups — not during the early mesolithic at least.

Base camps may have moved seasonally to take advantage of resources elsewhere, or to follow migrating herds of deer or aurochs. Communication between different groups must have been a frequent and routine activity, for the similarity of the material equipment throughout Britain suggests a common bond. This material equipment obviously varies according to the type of site (domestic base camp, hunters' camp, coastal settlement, toolmaking place, and so on), but mainly in the selection of suitable items from a traditional repertoire. The standardisation is remarkable, with few idiosyncrasies but for different shapes of microliths (see below). The later mesolithic of Ireland is an exception, possibly because of its insularity.

Mesolithic sites are to be found in Britain in almost every type of environment, although it is essential to visualise the environment as it was then. Pollen analysis shows that the early mesolithic population had to contend first with forests of pine, birch and hazel, the density of which would vary with the soils and topography. The climate was cooler than today, but drier. However, by the time of the later mesolithic an Atlantic climate produced a thick deciduous forest. Throughout the whole period, sites beside rivers or lakes were preferred, which is not surprising. Apart from fresh water, fish, waterfowl, natural pasture on flood plains and a varied hinterland, rivers offered relatively easy communication. Sites on light, particularly sandy, soils were popular, especially where they fringed chalk or clay lands. The chalk downland was less frequently used although it was often a source for flint. Caves and rock overhangs were sought for their natural shelter, especially in the Mendips and Derbyshire Peaks. Coastal sites with evidence of the exploitation of marine resources are not so common, but this must reflect the destruction of such sites where marine transgressions have occurred, which includes most of the English east and south coasts. The maps (figures 8 and 9) indicate some of the richer, well known mesolithic sites, all or most of which could be interpreted as base camps.

It is very difficult to estimate what quantities of food would need to be procured to feed a small group of mesolithic people as envisaged above, and to allow some to be stored for times of difficulty. There are too many unknown factors. It has been estimated that one red deer carcase would feed five people (two adults, three children) for ten days, presumably if it was not supplemented by other foodstuffs, which seems most unlikely. There are also some amusing statistics regarding the uneconomical nature of a shellfish diet, with one red-deer carcase being equivalent in food value to 52,267 oysters! Seven hundred oysters per day are quoted for survival in the absence of any other food, and 1400 cockles. Significantly, only four hundred limpets would be required. Any estimate must take into account the almost certainly low intake of carbohydrates, which feature so much in modern diets.

9. Map showing some later mesolithic sites, mostly referred to in the text.

Foraging

On the basis of ethnographic parallels it would not be surprising if the diet of mesolithic people consisted of a very high proportion of vegetable food in the form of nuts, fruits, leaves and edible roots. Unfortunately, although pollen analysis can show that many plants that could have been used as food were available in the right habitats, there is virtually nothing in the archaeological record to demonstrate that they were. Reed and bogbean, both of which have edible roots, grew at Star Carr, but it is rare that anything of this nature survives. The only exception is hazelnut. Burnt hazelnut shells have been found at many sites, preserved by the fact that they have been burnt. It is not too fanciful to picture people sitting around the embers of a fire, chewing the nuts and casting the shells into them. Their capacity for being stored for long periods must have made them a valuable item. As they could not be collected until the autumn, their presence on a site suggests occupation during winter or early spring.

There is almost nothing that survives that could be connected with what was probably a daily routine of collecting: baskets, carrying bags, digging sticks have understandably perished. A few flint flakes and blades occur with a characteristic polish on their cutting edges, which archaeologists refer to as 'sickle gloss'. The cutting of certain grasses does eventually impart such a gloss on flint, but even if this can be accepted as the real reason for the gloss such plant material may have been cut for bedding. No sickles have ever been found, such as were used by the mesolithic people of the Near East, although some of the slotted bones which held small flint blades in them, as found on the continent, may have served as sickles.

One form of tool which has been found in fair numbers, but usually in rivers with no context for dating them, is the perforated antler or bone mattock or pick. These may have been used for digging up roots and tubers. There are some from Star Carr of early mesolithic date. Other, rather simpler forms have come from the river Thames in the London area and radiocarbon dates indicate that they range from late mesolithic to neolithic. Examples are also known from the head of the Forth estuary near Stirling, on the Isle of Oronsay and a few other isolated sites. Also probably connected with digging were some of the so-called hourglass perforated pebble maceheads. These occur in considerable numbers, but usually as surface finds. Some would appear to be mesolithic, but they are also found in

10. (Left) Perforated antler-beam mattock dredged from the river Thames at Staines, Surrey, length 25 cm. (Photograph: Museum of London.)

11. (Below) Perforated 'macehead' of quartzite found in peat, probably of Boreal age, at a depth of 6 metres during the excavation for the Ocean Dock at Southampton. It was possibly used to weight a digging stick, as depicted in the adjacent South African rock painting. Diameter 9 cm.

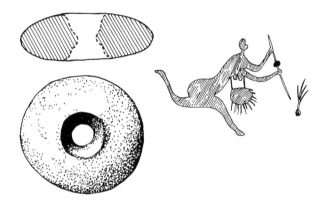

neolithic contexts. However, one from Southampton Dock is well dated to the late Boreal or early Post-boreal age by the peat in which it was found, 6 metres below present sea-level. They are usually made from carefully selected, flattish round pebbles of quartzite, and the boring of the perforation must have been a long and tedious task. A typical example is shown (figure 11) together with a vignette of a South African rock painting that shows such an object placed on a digging stick to give it extra weight. A woman is depicted with her carrying bag, digging out a plant. This does not imply that perforated pebble maceheads were not used for other purposes. Some have battered ends as if used as hammers.

It is impossible to know anything of the division of labour among the sexes in mesolithic times but, again to use ethnographic parallels, it does seem likely that foraging was one of the special roles of women, whereas the hunting of animals was a male prerogative. A better idea of the kind of diet that was enjoyed may be eventually given by the scientific study of

mesolithic human bones, for the composition of human bone
varies dependent on the proportions of vegetable, meat or fish
eaten over a period of time. This can only be determined by
meticulous isotope and trace element analysis. Experiments are
in progress: no positive results have yet been achieved but the
prospects appear to be good. However, such experiments have
to be conducted on the bones of continental mesolithic people
for, as will be seen in the next chapter, their skeletal remains in
Britain are very few.

Future research on sites with good organic preservation may,
by the application of wet-sieving techniques, eventually obtain
the evidence to confirm the probable use of a multitude of
plants and fruits in the mesolithic diet. At Morton, Fife, this was
done on a later mesolithic site. No abundance of material was
extracted, but a few seeds were found of some typical species of
waste land (chickweed, fat-hen, corn spurrey), all of which have
some food value. A sandstone pebble rubber or grinder was also
found at the same site and this may well have been used in the
preparation of such foodstuffs. A similar one was found at an
early mesolithic site in Norfolk. It is a type of tool that is not
easily identifiable and others may have been overlooked in the
past.

Hunting

Mesolithic people shared the land with a rich and varied
mammalian fauna, comprising animals which survived from Late
Glacial times and those which migrated across from the continent
as the climate ameliorated. Two of the great mammals of the
last ice age had become extinct: the woolly rhinoceros and the
woolly mammoth. Surprisingly, the mammoth did survive in
Britain until just into the Late Glacial, for in 1986 the skeleton
of one was found in Shropshire together with the remains of
three babies, in a deposit radiocarbon-dated to that time. The
giant deer or Irish elk had also become extinct. As the forest
canopy developed during the early mesolithic so reindeer and
horse disappeared elsewhere. Elk seems to have persisted until
about 6000 BC and aurochs into the neolithic period. All the
other animals are species living today, although a few are no
longer to be found in Britain, such as the wolf, brown bear, blue
hare and beaver.

As a predator, the mesolithic hunter had only one serious
competitor: the wolf. He had to be wary of packs of these
animals, and also of chance encounters with brown bears. How-

ever, apart from such hazards as vipers or being charged by a
bull aurochs or a wild boar, he had little to fear and, once
tracked down, his quarry was doomed. The danger was that the
indiscriminate slaughtering of beasts would lead to a serious
decrease in their numbers. Also, as the forest thickened, herds
of deer or aurochs probably split up into more but smaller
herds, reducing the hunters' chances of finding them or cutting
off stray animals.

Unfortunately, there are only three sites in Britain where
faunal remains have been found in sufficient numbers to give
some idea of what was hunted or, at times, possibly
scavenged: Star Carr, North Yorkshire; Thatcham, Berkshire;
and Morton, Fife. Deer, both red and roe, predominate. The
aurochs, a giant dangerous beast in comparison to modern
domesticated cattle, also occurs on these sites, as does elk. A
few horse teeth from Thatcham may emphasise the early
date, around 8000 bc or earlier for this site. All these
animals would have produced good meat, but much more is
provided: hides, bone and antler for tools and weapons,
sinew for bindings, stomachs and bladders for pouches and
containers, whiskers and teeth for personal ornaments. Other
animals found as bones on mesolithic sites, such as beaver,
pine marten, hare, wolf and fox, may have been hunted
specifically for their furs or pelts. They also give a good
idea of the surrounding environment; the beavers at Thatcham
must have created lakes which would have been beneficial to
themselves and to the local residents for the fish and
wildfowl they would have encouraged. A narrow channel at
the Thatcham site was originally thought to have been
artificially dug as a kind of fish trap, but it now seems much
more likely that it was a beaver-cut channel.

The technique of the mesolithic hunter can, to some extent,
be judged by the discarded equipment of the chase found on
almost all mesolithic sites, often in great quantity; this is
usually of flint, but also of bone and antler where conditions
have been suitable for its preservation. The most common
object is the microlith, a diagnostic hallmark of the period.
Usually no more than 2-4 cm long, they are made on
microblades of flint, shaped by further chipping along one or
more edges into various forms. The majority are pointed,
simply blunted obliquely across one end, or more elaborately
into triangles and crescents. Such points are characteristic of
the early mesolithic and the microliths generally become

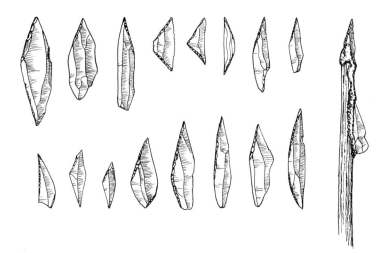

12. (Above and left) Earlier mesolithic microliths. (Top row) Thatcham, Berkshire; half size. (Bottom row) Oakhanger, Hampshire; half size. (Left) Bow with constricted grip from Holmegaard, Denmark; made of elm, about 1.5 metres long. (Right) Forepart of pine arrowshaft with microliths inset in resin; of early Boreal date from Loshult, Sweden; half size.

13. (Below) (From left to right) Four barbed antler points from Star Carr; harpoon of antler from Star Carr; bone point from Thatcham.

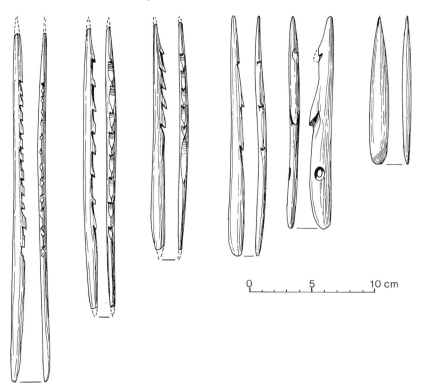

more geometric in shape and even smaller towards the later mesolithic. Some of the latter are extremely small, often of rod-like shape, and it is very difficult to know exactly what they were used for. However, there can be little doubt that the vast majority of the pointed forms at least were the composite armature of spears or arrows, set in slots as barbs, and secured with resin, as has been rarely preserved on some microliths. A typical range of microlith forms is illustrated (figure 12), as also is a rare Swedish find of a pine arrowshaft with one microlith set as a barb behind the pointed end. Identical use of such microlithic armature by San bushmen in southern Africa or present-day Masai people in Tanzania (although the latter use cut tinplate for their barb instead of stone) makes it almost certain that it was for the same purpose, namely the application of poison to the barb. Poison is not applied to the actual point of the arrow because rapid selection from a quiver could result in a fatal prick to the thumb or finger. Also, the barb ensures that even if the arrow does not penetrate the body of the quarry, it could well graze the skin and impart the poison into the bloodstream. Furthermore, any such cuts might produce a blood spoor which could be followed until eventually the exhausted, poisoned animal could be found and despatched. Microliths set as barbs along the shaft of a spear would serve the same purpose. The delicate barbs would frequently break when the thrown spear missed its target and struck something hard such as stones in the ground. Many of the flint concentrations found in Britain could well be explained as temporary camps where flint was gathered and made into microliths, to repair spears and arrows. Nothing has ever been found which could indicate what poison may have been used, but such substances as adder venom and deadly nightshade were available. The use of bows is proved by the discovery of them on some Danish waterlogged sites, where remarkable finds have been made of objects made of such materials as wood, bone and even textiles, string and rope. No mesolithic sites with such superb survival of organic material have yet been examined in Britain; Star Carr has produced comparable material, but no bow.

Another traditional piece of hunting equipment during the Late Glacial and early mesolithic periods was the barbed point of bone or antler, a form of weapon that dates back to the Magdalenian phase of the French Upper Palaeolithic. One, dredged from the present floor of the North Sea, has already been illustrated. There are variations in the form with barbs on

both sides or only one side (biserial or uniserial respectively),
the manner in which the barbs have been cut and the fine or
wide spacing of the barbs. The length of the shafts behind the
barbs also varies and all these things can be interpreted as
implying different functions, local traditions or development
through time. They are often referred to as harpoons, but unless
there is some apparent method of attaching a line, such as a
hole or projection at the base, they are best referred to as
barbed points. All the British examples are of uniserial type,
with the exception of two Late Glacial ones from Aveline's Hole
in the Mendips and Kent's Cavern near Torquay, Devon.

The distribution of barbed points is predominantly on the east
side of Britain, particularly in Yorkshire. They are always found
in lakeside or riverside contexts, but this may reflect the conditions suitable for their preservation. Two broken ones have been
dredged from the river Thames at Battersea and Wandsworth
in London, and two others were found in an old channel of the
river Gipping near Ipswich, Suffolk. Apart from those mentioned
above from the West Country, there are two exceptions to the
eastern distribution: one from near Oswestry, Shropshire, and
another at Poulton-le-Fylde, Lancashire. Neither area is rich in
mesolithic or Late Glacial finds, but the latter site in an old lake
basin is of especial interest because it proves that such weapons
were used for hunting large game, for two broken barbed points
were found in contact with the skeleton of an elk. The beast had
presumably swum into the water with the points embedded in its
body and drowned, never to be recovered by its hunters. Lesions
on the bones indicate previous attacks on the beast. Injuries to
the legs, if intentional, have been postulated as attempts to
secure the animal alive, possibly to facilitate transport of it back
to a base camp.

Star Carr, another lakeside site, produced nearly two hundred
barbed points when excavated in 1949-51. Nearly all of them
were made of antler. Only one could be identified as a true
harpoon with a perforation halfway down the tang; otherwise
they would presumably have been mounted as spearheads on
wooden shafts. Bindings of thread and the use of adhesive resin
can be seen on some Swedish examples, and two of the Star
Carr barbed points had resin still adhering to their tangs. Some
may have been mounted in pairs, with the barbs facing each
other, to form leister prongs as used by Eskimoes for fishing (see
below). The disappearance from mesolithic sites of barbed points
of this Late Glacial and early mesolithic type from about 7000 bc

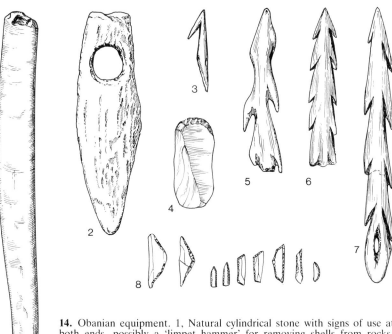

14. Obanian equipment. 1, Natural cylindrical stone with signs of use at both ends, possibly a 'limpet hammer' for removing shells from rocks; Oronsay. 2, Perforated antler mattock; Oronsay. 3, Fish-hook, probably made from a broken bone point; Risga Island. 4, Flint scraper; Jura. 5, Barbed bone point; Oronsay. 6, Barbed bone point; Oronsay. 7, Barbed bone harpoon; Oban. 8, Microliths; Jura. (All half size.)

is puzzling, and very different forms of barbed points appear in the later mesolithic, found in Scotland at Oban and on some of the offshore islands such as Oronsay (figure 14). They are flattish, with biserial barbs in most cases. As they were found at coastal sites, it seems very likely that they were used as fish spears. A couple of stray finds of biserial barbed points in Ayrshire and Kirkcudbrightshire may be related, as is another from the shore at Whitburn in Tyne and Wear. Another puzzling feature is the absence of any barbed points at Thatcham in the Kennet valley. A few bone points were found which were probably spearheads but nothing comparable to Star Carr, which is broadly contemporary. This may be merely a reflection on the sparseness of the material from Thatcham.

There are some other clues, apart from the hunting equipment, to the hunting practices of the mesolithic: one is the mounting

Mesolithic Britain

evidence for the intentional burning of scrubland or forest to create open areas, and another is the presence of the dog, the only animal definitely known to have been domesticated in the period. British examples of the mesolithic dog are restricted to one femur from Thatcham and part of a skull and maxilla from Star Carr. The skull of a more complete example was more recently found at the early mesolithic site of Bedburg-Konigshoven in the valley of the Rhine, Germany. It can only be assumed that dogs were employed in the hunt, but they would clearly have helped considerably, especially in frightening animals away from the main body of a herd. This could have been

15. (Below and bottom) Skull of a dog from an earlier mesolithic site at Bedburg in the Rhine valley, Germany, length 157 mm. (Photographs: Romisch-Germanisches Zentralmuseum, taken from M. Street, 1989, Jager and Schamanen, RGZM Mainz.)

part of a conscious plan to avoid disturbing a whole herd, especially of deer, and causing them all to flee. By creating minimal disturbance it was much more likely that the animals would regard the hunters as a normal part of their life. Similarly, a study of the faunal remains from Star Carr indicates that red and roe deer were selectively culled at the age of three and one years respectively in order to maintain a balance of numbers in a herd. Added to this management of deer herds is the activity of keeping areas open by burning. This is confirmed by pollen diagrams which show distinct evidence of clearing in association with charcoal and mesolithic artefacts in the soil profile at the same level. The most informative site of this nature is White Gill at a height of about 400 metres OD on the Yorkshire Moors above the head of Westerdale. It is a late mesolithic site with large numbers of microliths, no axes and hardly any other tools. It is considered that the blanket peat now covering the moor is a direct result of the modification of the vegetation cover, changing the whole drainage pattern and thus causing peat to form. If this is so, it implies that mesolithic hunters were responsible for the open character of the moors today, at White Gill and many other places, for the forest was unable to regenerate on the peat.

The advantages of burning off the vegetation on poor soils are numerous, as can be seen after any heath fire at the present day: gorse, bracken and other scrub are mainly removed and the hunters' mobility is increased, but even more important is that next spring there will be a carpet of succulent young shoots to attract and nourish deer or other browsing animals. It also means that the hunters know where they are likely to find the animals and, as a bonus, the growth of hazel is encouraged as it is 'fire-tolerant', thus assuring a valuable supply of nuts for the future. It would therefore seem that the mesolithic hunter had achieved a relationship with herds of deer instead of roaming in the hope of a chance quarry. The line between this and domestication is a thin one and it is perhaps emphasised by the discovery at two sites in southern England, Oakhanger in Hampshire and Winfrith Heath in Dorset, of large quantities of ivy pollen in the soil profile, far more than could be accounted for by natural reasons. Ivy must have been brought to the site purposely, and in winter after it had flowered otherwise there would not have been any pollen from it. Ivy is very palatable to red deer so perhaps it was intended to attract them or even feed tethered animals.

The sandy areas of the Weald of south-east England would, like the Yorkshire Moors, have responded well to deliberate clearance by fire. Nor is it likely to be a coincidence that the pollen diagram from Hockham Mere in East Anglia shows a peak at the same level which is interpreted as a forest clearance in the late mesolithic. Hockham Mere, too, is in an area of poor sandy 'Breckland' soil, but clearly this form of management cannot have been used over the vast areas of dense forest on heavier soils, the ideal habitat of the wild boar which feature strongly in the mesolithic diet. One can only guess that they were hunted with throwing and thrusting spears.

Fishing and fowling

Fish, molluscs, crustaceans, land and sea birds all added to the mesolithic food supply, in varying quantities according to circumstances. The marine resources were the most important. Sometimes coastal sites seem to have been temporary or seasonal settlements; at other times it appears that the exploitation of fish and shellfish was a major element in the economy. Also, the preference for inland sites beside rivers and lakes was presumably encouraged by the constant presence of waterfowl and fish, although the latter may have been very scarce at the beginning of the mesolithic period. For instance, no fish remains were found at Star Carr, in spite of the meticulous excavation and sieving, and there was only one fish vertebra from Thatcham. The reason for this does not appear to be either a lack of angling prowess or unsuitable conditions for the preservation of fish bones. It would seem that during the peak of the last glaciation, about twenty to eighteen thousand years ago, the climate killed off all the fish in the British freshwater streams and it took several thousand years for various species to recolonise them. Both Star Carr and Thatcham are very early mesolithic sites (eighth millennium bc) and the fish had not then returned in any numbers, if at all further up the river valleys. However, birds were widely available and there are a fair number of avian remains on both of these sites which must represent kills or trappings. They give a vivid picture of the surroundings: crane, teal or garganey, mallard, goldeneye duck and possibly smew at Thatcham; crane, white stork, great and little grebe, pintail, red-breasted merganser, red-throated diver, lapwing and buzzard at Star Carr.

Nothing is known of the manner in which the earlier mesolithic population may have exploited seafood for this was a time of low sea-level and any coastal sites of that time now lie under the present sea or, more likely, were destroyed by the waves as the sea-level gradually rose. By comparison, several later mesolithic sites do survive. Their distribution is almost entirely restricted to south-western England and western Scotland. For the most part these sites are scatters or dumps of marine shells, mixed with mesolithic artefacts and occasional bones or other objects. At Westward Ho! in Devon such a midden rests on estuarine clay and is covered by peat dated to the fifth millennium bc. Oysters, mussels, limpets and winkles had been collected in quantity. Blashenwell in Dorset is another site of about the same date but, unlike Westward Ho!, which is on the present sea shore, it is 3 km from the sea, yet limpets and winkles had been carried there. This is unusual, for shellfish collecting was usually done from a base beside or at least close to the sea — certainly if the shellfish were regarded as an essential item for survival during certain periods of the year. Thus sites were generally chosen on small islands as this meant a longer coastline within easy reach. It has already been mentioned what vast quantities of shellfish are required if they are to be regarded as a substantial proportion of one's daily food. Large loads of shellfish are heavy so it is not surprising that the lighter winkles and limpets predominate over whelks and oysters. Also, limpets have a greater food value.

There is only one coastal site in southern England which has been excavated to good archaeological standards and can thus give a more detailed picture of the use of marine resources in the mesolithic: Culver Well on the Isle of Portland, Dorset. It is a rich site and will be mentioned again in the next chapter for the evidence it has for the actual settlement, but its importance as a centre for the exploitation of shellfish is relevant here. It consists of a large midden of shells, not very high but spread out, with a substantial floor of limestone slabs placed over part of it. There is a large cooking pit, about a metre wide and as deep, a hearth and at least one posthole. This was clearly not a short-lived, temporary site, even if it may have been used only at certain times of the year. On the higher ground above the cliffs, it is set back from the coast by about 0.5 km, perhaps in order to make the journeys to other parts of the island shorter. No fish bones were found, in spite of sieving, and very few mammalian bones. Winkles and limpets predominated but some crabs had been collected. The base of the midden has been radiocarbon-dated to 5200 ± 135 bc. The stonework includes normal forms of tools and microliths and a crude form of pick in large

16. Pick made of Portland chert; Culver Well, Portland, Dorset. Half size.

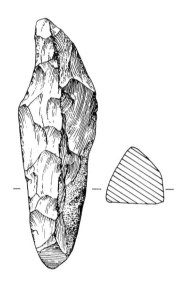

numbers (more than two hundred) that is peculiar to the site and immediate area. These picks are made of the local Portland chert, as are most of the other artefacts, but it is difficult to know what they were used for. Experiments have shown that they are no more effective for knocking limpets off rocks than a suitably sized pebble. Many show battering at one end but whether they were hafted or held in the hand is unknown. One likely possibility is that they were used to prize out the valuable blocks of tabular Portland chert from local rock exposures, exploited for making tools and weapons and transported in small quantities over much of southern England. This would explain the excessive numbers of these picks in comparison to the few examples found on other sites.

   The location of this site at Culver Well, close to the Fleet, a basin of water between the Chesil Bank and the mainland to the north-west of Portland Bill, suggests that it may have been the centre for a coastal economy having connections with many of the numerous mesolithic sites of Dorset that are often within walking distance of the sea. An even clearer illustration of organised adaptation to marine resources is found at a series of later mesolithic sites on the mainland of Scotland and some of the islands off the west coast, particularly around Oban and on Jura and Oronsay. Several sites on the latter island have been excavated and studied, and there is a good case for concluding that the inhabitants stayed permanently on the island, moving occasionally from one site to another, but supplementing their diet with meat from the mainland, importing it with other useful items such as deer antler for making tools. Apart from the ubiquitous limpets, analysis of fish bones has shown that 90 per cent of them were from the tasty saithe or coalfish. Sea fish were also very well represented on the island of Risga, with skate, conger eel, grey mullet and haddock included. This raises the question of fishing practices. Barbed bone spearheads were certainly used in shallow water, but these species must indicate the use of some form of boat, line-fishing or netting. Nets are known from comparable sites in Denmark, where waterlogged deposits have preserved such items. Nothing of this nature has yet been found in Britain, and only one fish-hook is known from Oronsay, apparently made from a broken barbed bone point. Continental parallels also suggest that boats may have been made of skins stretched over light wooden frames, similar to a coracle. Such would probably be more seaworthy than the one example of a dugout canoe that is radiocarbon-dated to this period, from Friarton, Perth. It was made of pine wood, 4.50 metres long and 1.00 metre wide, the hollowed-out part being 1.80 metres long and 0.60 metre deep. This had been laboriously cut out by burning and scraping.

These Scottish mesolithic coastal sites also produce remains of

17. Excavation of Cnoc Coig, Oronsay, revealing the hearth of burnt stones and shell midden in section. (Photograph: P. Mellars.)

18. Close-up of shells in the Caisteal nau Gilleau midden, Oronsay. (Photograph: P. Mellars.)

seabirds, including on Risga the extinct giant auk. There is no evidence for seal-hunting as there is in the Scandinavian late mesolithic, but it seems that occasional stranded whales were taken advantage of, for their remains have been found in the valley of the Forth associated with antler tools that could have been used to butcher them. A typical midden on the Isle of Oronsay is illustrated in figures 17 and 18.

One of the earliest eastern Scottish sites is Morton near the mouth of the Firth of Tay. It is now 4 km inland but when occupied (around 4300-5300 bc but probably earlier as well) the sea-level was higher and it was an island linked to the mainland only at low tide. The occupants practised a mixed economy, hunting an occasional red and roe deer, aurochs and pig, all presumably killed nearby as the whole of their skeletons is represented. Whelks and mussels were the most commonly eaten shellfish. Many seabirds were caught, and a few land birds such as thrush and crow. Among a number of deep-sea fish consumed cod was the most important. This could have been obtained only some distance from the shore in a boat.

5
Lifestyle

We have already seen that the most likely pattern of existence was the establishment of base camps by small groups of a few families and a fairly regular routine of foraging and hunting, as much as possible being conducted within daily reach of the camp. Some of the men would frequently be away for days on forays but, at times of abundance, would presumably assist with collecting the valuable fruits and nuts that could be stored. Meat and fish could also be dried and smoked in order to provide security for the group against lean times. Such activities, and the routine preparation and cooking of food at the camp, required the constant collection of firewood and water. The known sites are generally close to fresh water, but some sort of container would be required to carry water as well as boil it for cooking. Leather bags or animal bladders would be suitable for the former but no such items have survived. However, cooking pits have been identified, as at Culver Well, Portland, Dorset, where a large pit is thought to have been used for cooking large quantities of food by placing it on and between hot stones and covering it with earth or turves and leaving it to smoulder for several hours. Wild boar or roebuck would do very well, cooked whole, in this manner. Otherwise, occasional small pits on mesolithic sites may have had some form of lining placed in them so that they held water. Hot flints from the fire, placed in the water, would soon bring it to the boil and it could be kept simmering by throwing in additional ones. Small flint stones, heated and put into water, crack and hiss and soon become white and crazed. These so-called 'pot-boilers' occur frequently on mesolithic sites, as they do on many later prehistoric ones.

The camp would have been a busy place, when fully occupied, with old equipment being repaired and new being made. Ethnographical parallels suggest that the people would have entertained themselves with story-telling, music, singing and dancing. The nature of social contacts with other groups can only be guessed. Accidental encounters between foragers and hunters must have occurred, but meetings may have been contrived at certain seasons of the year at particular places, and perhaps even presents exchanged to encourage friendship, marriage partners sought and events discussed. Apart from a pitifully small number of exotic objects that sometimes occur on mesolithic

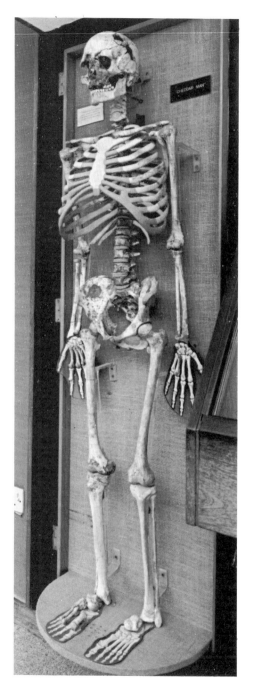

19. 'Cheddar Man': the most complete human skeleton found of the mesolithic period, dated to about 7150 bc. It was discovered in 1903 in the entrance to Gough's Cave in Cheddar Gorge, Somerset, and is now displayed in the Cheddar Show Caves Museum. (Photograph: Cheddar Show Caves.)

sites (pieces of Portland chert and siltstone rubbers or pounders from the coast, for instance, at Farnham, Surrey, and elsewhere, very distant from their source), there is virtually no archaeological evidence to support this. Indeed, everything stated above is mainly supposition, so it is better to look at the objects which have been found and relate them as well as possible to the life of the people. This is done briefly below under appropriate headings. Archaeological features, in the sense of pits, postholes or any other artificial disturbance of the ground, are also examined. Firstly, however, we shall consider what is known about the physical nature of the people themselves, deduced from the scanty skeletal remains that have been found.

Human burials

Human skeletal remains from the whole of the mesolithic period are so rare in Britain and, except for two sites in the Mendips, so incomplete that little can be said other than that it was a normal human population of modern type that is represented. Whether the people were generally tall or stocky, broad or thin-faced, or had any characteristics differing much from our own is unknown. There is no reason to think there was anything about them we should now consider unusual and, even if there was a rich collection of skeletons to study, it would still not tell us whether the people were usually blond or dark or the colour of their eyes.

There are a few cave sites with skeletal remains that can, with varying degrees of confidence, be related to the Late Glacial period: Robin Hood's Cave and Pin Hole Cave at Creswell Crags, Derbyshire/Nottinghamshire; most of the material from Gough's Cave and some skull fragments from Flint Jack's Cave, both at Cheddar, Somerset; and a male adult and a child's skull from Langwith Cave, Derbyshire. Radiocarbon dates have shown that the complete skeleton found at Gough's Cave, now exhibited at the site and referred to as 'Cheddar Man', is not of later Upper Palaeolithic date as originally thought. The new method of radiocarbon dating, which can be done with minute amounts of bone (thus not necessitating the partial destruction of precious specimens), has shown that 'Cheddar Man' is of mesolithic date (7150 ± 100 bc), and it is the most complete skeleton known for the period in Britain. It is the skeleton of a young adult male. Not far from Cheddar is Burrington Coombe, containing a cave known as Aveline's Hole. Multiple burials were found here in 1805 and it was reported that there were fifty skeletons placed parallel to each other. A fine biserial barbed point and Cres-wellian-type flintwork suggested a later Upper Palaeolithic date for the burials. Unfortunately the remains of only nine of these skeletons are preserved; twenty were destroyed by an air raid on Bristol in 1941 and the others have been lost. Some new radiocarbon dates obtained from the preserved bones are, like Gough's Cave, also of mesolithic date (7150 ± 100 bc and 6910 ± 100 bc) and, in view of the manner in which the bodies had been placed, date the whole cemetery. Grave goods seem to have been limited to some worked bone, teeth, a winkle shell and a fossil ammonite. The top of a child's skull is said to have been put upside down by the shoulder of one of the skeletons.

These mesolithic burials from the Mendips are difficult to explain as the only other human bones in Britain, other than some very late ones from Scotland mentioned below, are a humerus from Thatcham, Berkshire, another humerus from the same cave at Paviland, West Glamorgan, which produced the famous but much earlier 'Red Lady of Paviland', some fragments from Kent's Cavern (Devon), Badger Hole in the Mendips, Prestatyn (Clwyd), Three Holes Cave at Torbryan (Devon), and a skull of doubtful date from the river Yare at Strumpshaw, Norfolk. A likely explanation is that the cave burials were perpetuating a custom evident in the earlier Creswellian, for there were other burials at Gough's Cave dated to around 10,500 bc. Some of these had been rather gruesomely dis-membered and defleshed.

Although the skeletal material is so little, its very sparseness tells us something of the manner in which the dead were disposed. Burial as such, excluding caves, could not have existed without some having been discovered by now. It is probable that dead bodies were exposed in isolated places. Carnivores, birds and chemical decay would soon have removed all trace and left nothing for the archaeologist.

Some human remains have come from a few sites around Oban, Argyll, associated with the 'Obanian' late mesolithic. At the MacKay Cave partial skeletons of a man and a child were found with those of a dog; four individuals, three of them male, came from MacArthur Cave but are possibly younger than the Obanian; four adults and four children in the Distillery Cave at Oban may also not belong with the Obanian midden, which was indiscriminately emptied — this was very unfortunate for the skeletons had the narrow type of skull often associated with the later neolithic population of Britain.

20. Shelter or house. Plan of post and stake holes as excavated at Broom Hill, Braishfield, Hampshire. The posts probably held timbers which supported skins or some other form of roof covering. Some of the stake holes may have held pegs to secure the posts or roof coverings.

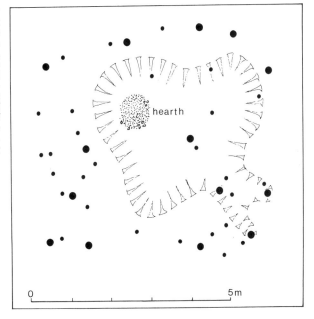

Dwellings and other structures

The excavation of mesolithic sites sometimes reveals post or stake holes, scooped hollows and pits, stone paving and hearth or spreads of charcoal. Rarely is it possible to interpret these features with confidence, but undoubtedly some of them relate to the construction of simple shelters. There are also natural hollows, cave mouths and rock shelters which had been used. Concentrations of flint waste associated with hearths may well mark the spots where tent-like structures once stood, too flimsy to leave any permanent evidence in the soil.

The most convincing record of a dwelling structure is from a late mesolithic site at Broom Hill, Braishfield, near Romsey in Hampshire: post and stake holes surround an artificial hollow with a central post and internal hearth. A series of stake holes on another late mesolithic site at Downtown, near Salisbury, Wiltshire, is considered to belong to two very small structures (about 1.50 metres across) with vertical stakes possibly pulled and bound together at the top to make a frame for some covering. Supporting this interpretation are a few other stake holes outside, purposely set in the ground leaning away from the framework, just as we would insert tent pegs. In Ireland, at Mount Sandal in County Derry, there is a complex of postholes and stakes around and in a natural hollow, associated with hearths. This gives the impression of a series of buildings and demolitions over a period of time. The site was occupied during the earlier Irish mesolithic, around 7000-6500 bc. On the Yorkshire Moors, strategically placed close to one of the lowest crossing places on the Pennines, two shelters have been found: one on Bromehead Moor consisted of five stake holes enclosing an area 5.00 by 3.30 metres. The roughly paved interior was covered with charcoal as if the shelter had burnt down. At Dunford Bridge, South Yorkshire, there was just an oval patch

21. Vertical view of the post and stake holes of a mesolithic hut and associated features at Mount Sandal, County Derry, Ireland. (Photograph: P. Woodman.)

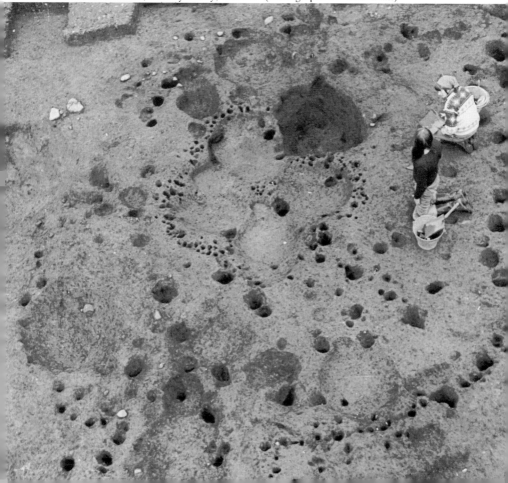

22. Culver Well, Isle of Portland, Dorset. Excavation showing the extensive floor of limestone slabs. The cliff edge is visible in the background. (Photograph: S. L. Palmer.)

of stones 2.60 metres across but no trace of stake holes. An unusual feature of this site was a large stone mounted on vertical flagstones for use as a table or anvil. Cobbles or flagstones were also used in a structure at Deepcar in South Yorkshire. Associated with some of the coastal mesolithic sites along the Solway Firth are natural hollows or scoops with a few stake holes. Other stake-hole features, as on the middens on the island of Oronsay, surrounding areas of burning, were more likely connected with the smoking of fish. Also in Scotland, but in the east at Morton, Fife, possible shelters were identified, and a line of stake holes probably forming a windbreak.

The use of stone paving, already mentioned, is best demonstrated on the impressive site at Culver Well on the Isle of Portland, Dorset. Here a well laid floor of local limestone slabs had been placed over and around a shell midden. Only one posthole was found, and that may be connected with the preserving of fish, possibly filleted on the beach as no fish bones were found. Alternatively, it could have been a support for some dwelling structure which has left no other trace. At Newferry, County Antrim, a later Irish mesolithic site in the Bann valley, layers of stones had been placed on the underlying peat to stabilise it. A more substantial stone pavement was placed around one of the Solway Firth sites at Barsalloch. A very different kind of flooring was found at Williamson's Moss, Eskmeals, on the Cumbrian coast: birch bark laid over brushwood to counteract the damp conditions. Another floor of sandstone slabs and pebbles laid in a rectangle, associated with a tent-like structure, has been found at Greasby on Merseyside, apparently of earlier mesolithic date.

Apart from those briefly mentioned above, numerous hollows have been identified as sites of mesolithic habitation, as at Farnham in Surrey, White Colne in Essex and others. Unless they are surrounded by stake holes, like one at Wakeford's Copse, Havant, Hampshire, and the others mentioned, it is just as likely they were quarries for good-quality flint. Also, many of the reported hollows are clearly natural features and it may just have been that they made convenient places for an occasional fire. However, the two sites at Selmeston, East Sussex, and

23. Williamson's Moss, Eskmeals, Cumbria. Wooden structural remains as revealed by excavation. Timber lattice and decayed brushwood covering shows in the bottom left corner. (Photograph: C. Bonsall.)

Abinger, Surrey, often referred to as 'pit dwellings', are different; the hollows are artificial but very steep and narrow with no floor space. If they were used for habitation, it can only have been for sleeping in.

There is a site on Stoney Low in the Derbyshire Peaks where a natural recess in the limestone has been modified with a line of rocks, some cobbling and the erection of an isolated upright stone which served either as a seat or as an anvil, for struck flints lay around it. Timbers may have been put across the recess to support some covering. Some horse remains and a few Creswellian-type flints indicate that this may have been a Late Glacial or very early mesolithic site.

There are several caves in the Mendips, the Gower Peninsula and the Peak District of Derbyshire with scatters of mesolithic flints, suggesting brief visits for temporary shelter. Especially interesting are numerous outcrops of sandstone in the Weald that were used for shelter by mesolithic groups, some possibly as base camps, such as at Stonewall Park, Chiddingstone, Kent. Other sites have been excavated at High Rocks near Tunbridge Wells. Only later mesolithic material has so far been found at these natural rock shelters.

Crafts

Without suitably made tools of flint it would have been impossible to perform a multitude of tasks and, equally important, work and shape other materials such as wood, antler, bone, hide and much else which has perished. *Flintworking* was thus the most important craft, essential to the whole economy and life pattern of mesolithic groups. The consistent skill and manner in which the flint, or occasionally other suitable stone, was flaked or knapped, with rigid standardised methods, shows that this was the work of specialists within any group. As with any traditional craft, they would have been trained by the previous generation of specialists and would pass it on to the next. Never on mesolithic sites does one find the clumsy remains of haphazard 'do-it-yourself' methods. Obtaining good flint was not an easy task in a richly vegetated landscape and it would be surprising if there were not various restrictions or taboos on the use of it. Mention has been made of artificial hollows on gravel sites possibly for the extraction of flint. There was also one close to the shelters identified at Downton, Wiltshire. Natural solution hollows in chalk, as on the South Downs around Butser Hill, Hampshire, have mesolithic flintwork in their fillings and were apparently being exploited for the fresh flint nodules that were exposed. On the Pennines of Yorkshire a white flint was used almost exclusively on the early mesolithic sites, and the only known source of this flint, apart from glacially transported erratics, is in Lincolnshire, so expeditions to known sources must have been a routine activity in most parts of Britain. Inferior material, such as beach pebbles, was used when nothing else was available, and the products suffered accordingly.

For all the light tools required, blades of flint were struck in a very systematic manner from prepared cores, by direct or indirect percussion, as is shown diagrammatically (figure 24). This produced immediate knives or blanks for retouching into various tool forms such as scrapers, burins and borers. The very

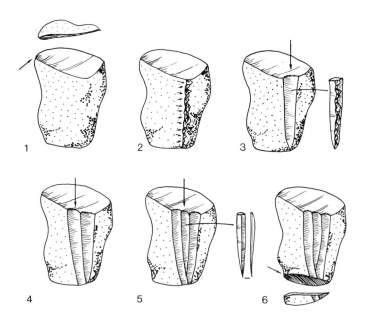

24. The technique for the production of flint blades: 1, removal of a flake from an unworked nodule to produce a striking platform; 2, chipping along a suitable edge to form a straight ridge; 3, removal of a flake from the striking platform down the straight edge, resulting in a distinctive 'crested flake' — sometimes double-crested if the straight ridge is formed by flaking from both sides; 4-5, successive removals of blades either by direct percussion or with a bone or antler punch; 6, removal of a flake to produce another striking platform at the opposite end on the core if practical, so that blades may be struck from two directions. A distinctive 'core tablet' is produced if further flakes are removed across the striking platform, often done to maintain the correct angle or rectify damage to the core by mis-hits.

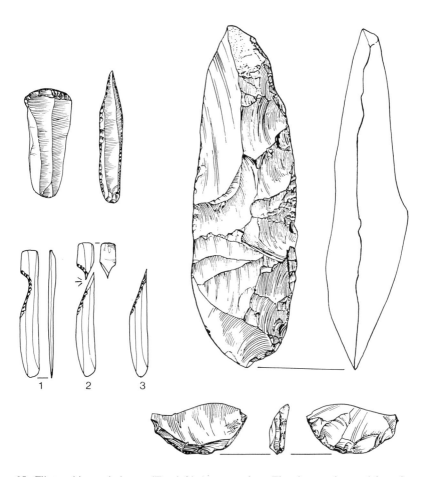

25. Flintworking techniques. (Top left) A scraper from Thatcham and an awl from Star Carr. Such tools were simply made by chipping selected blades or flakes around their edges to the desired shape. (Bottom left) Microlith manufacture. In order to make the point at the thickest, bulbar end of the blade (the end where it had been struck) for strength, a notch was chipped out (1) and the bulbar end snapped off obliquely (2) and then the point finally trimmed (3). The waste piece is referred to as a micro-burin. (Right) A tranchet axe, so called because of the final transverse flake struck across the cutting edge. Resharpening in the same manner produced distinctive axe-sharpening flakes as below. Many of these axes were really adzes, in that they were hafted with the cutting edge at right angles to the axis of the shaft. The axe and sharpening flake illustrated come from Great Melton, Norfolk. All half size.

small 'microblades' were the blanks for making microliths. These were made by an ingenious method of notching and snapping off the thick end of the microblade where it had been struck, and doing this obliquely so that only a little further chipping or blunting was necessary to complete a microlithic point. The purpose of this was to ensure that the point was at the thick end so that, as a barb inserted into a spear, it would be strong. The waste piece, known as a micro-burin, is as diagnostic of mesolithic flintwork as are the microliths.

Heavy tools such as axeheads were manufactured by a different technique, working down a nodule of flint by direct percussion with hard stone hammers, generally finishing with soft bar hammers of antler, bone or boxwood. The cutting edges of the finished axes were produced by a transverse flake and, when the axe became blunt through use, another such flake was removed to resharpen it. The axe-resharpening flake is very distinctive. These heavy tools vary in size from a few centimetres in length to 20 cm or more, clearly intended for different purposes. Also, many of these axes were almost certainly mounted in hafts with the cutting edge at right angles to the major axis of the haft and should therefore be called adzes. There is not a single example on any mesolithic site of the cutting edge of any flint axe or adze being sharpened by grinding, as done by later neolithic people, but at Nab Head, Dyfed, and in Ireland at Newferry, County Antrim, some axes have been found that were made by grinding suitably elongated pebbles of mudstone or other fine-grained rocks. Also in Ireland, a flaked and polished axe of volcanic

26. Cut marks on timber from Williamson's Moss, Eskmeals, Cumbria. (Photograph: J. Rock.)

27. Felled birch tree, Star Carr, North Yorkshire. (Photograph: Professor J. G. D. Clarke and Cambridge University Museum of Archaeology and Anthropology.)

rock comes from a late mesolithic site at Ferriters Cove, County Kerry.

The heavy so-called tranchet axes, named after the sharpening process, were presumably used for felling trees and working the obtained timber. Characteristic cut marks can be seen on a piece of oak from the Eskmeals site, and axe marks on a felled birch tree at Star Carr. Wood must have been used not only for frameworks for shelters and for other heavier items from dugout canoes to walkways but also for a great variety of small articles in everyday use. In Britain these have all perished, apart from part of a paddle of birchwood and the remains of a shaft in the perforation of an antler mattock, both from Star Carr. On the continent bows, arrows and even barbed points of wood have been found.

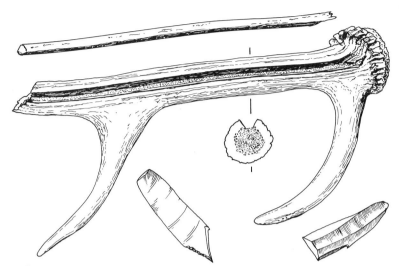

28. The groove and splinter technique for producing blanks for barbed points or other implements. Grooves were cut along an antler beam, close to and parallel with each other, through the hard outer part, until they reached the soft spongy interior. The required splinter could then be levered or prized out. The grooves were made with flint burins; two typical ones are illustrated.

Second to flint, the working of *antler and bone* was important, especially for barbed points, knives, awls and mattocks. This often entailed the preparation of long splinters as blanks, and these were extracted from the beams of antlers by cutting parallel grooves along them, through the bony exterior into the spongy inner cavity. It is then possible to extract a splinter which can be worked with flint blades. The heavy cutting edges of burins were ideal for cutting the grooves and examination of the microwear imparted on them at Star Carr supports this. The same technique was also used on bone.

Leatherworking must also have occupied much time, from the preparation of the hides to the finished products. Again, one can only guess at what was made as not a single leather object has survived. Flint scrapers are the commonest tools on all later stone age sites, including mesolithic ones. As the name suggests,

29. Grooved antler beam from which a splinter has been partly extracted; Star Carr, North Yorkshire. (Photograph: Cambridge University Museum of Archaeology and Anthropology.)

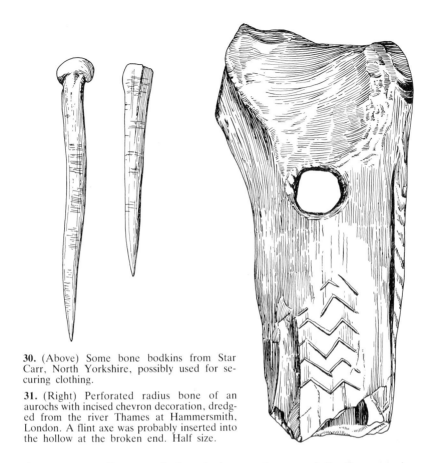

30. (Above) Some bone bodkins from Star Carr, North Yorkshire, possibly used for securing clothing.

31. (Right) Perforated radius bone of an aurochs with incised chevron decoration, dredged from the river Thames at Hammersmith, London. A flint axe was probably inserted into the hollow at the broken end. Half size.

they are usually regarded as being made especially for scraping hides. They are certainly very good for this and microwear studies on the Star Carr scrapers indicate that 40 per cent of them were used for this purpose, but others were used for working bone, wood and antler, so the scraper was really a general-purpose tool. Of all the uses of leather, which include tent coverings, bags and water carriers, cooking vessels and wrappings or bindings, clothing and footwear must have been the main ones. The only clues to the type of clothing that was worn are a few bone pins or bodkins possibly used to fasten the fronts of shoulder coverings or tunics.

In the waterlogged sites of Denmark and other places in northern Europe fine examples of *netting* and *basketry* have survived and it is inconceivable that these crafts were not practised in Britain. *Birch bark* was also used both as a source of resin and for making small vessels. Canoes, also, may have been made with it. Many rolls of birch bark of different widths were found at Star Carr, but nothing made from them. The only evidence for personal decoration comes from several discoveries of perforated shells, teeth and small worked or unworked pieces of shale and amber that were presumably *beads*, strung as necklaces or attached to clothing. A number of perforated cowrie shells came from one of the middens on the Isle of Oronsay. Pierced winkle shells were found at Culver Well, Portland, and shale beads at Star Carr and at Nab Head, Dyfed. At the latter site over sixty such beads were found and were being manufactured there.

Art and magic

There is nothing in Britain that can certainly be regarded as contemporary with the geometric and schematic decoration found on some Danish mesolithic objects, or with the delightful little animal figurines made of amber in the Copenhagen Museum, also thought to be mesolithic. The only British piece that might qualify is the perforated distal end of an aurochs radius from the river Thames at Hammersmith, London. Although undated, it bears the same type of ornamentation as found on some of the Danish examples, but decoration of a

32. A small pit found beneath the limestone floor at Culver Well, Portland, Dorset, containing a scallop shell, an axe and a small cylindrical pebble. The large pebble on the left side lay beside the capstone covering the pit. (Photograph: S. L. Palmer.)

33. Stag antlers with perforated frontlets from Bedburg in the Rhine valley, Germany, identical to those found at Star Carr, North Yorkshire. (Photograph: taken from M. Street, 1989, Jager and Schamanen, RGZM Mainz.)

similar kind does occasionally occur on later neolithic objects. For this reason a decorated antler tine found near Romsey, Hampshire, has been discounted as necessarily mesolithic.

An unusual discovery was made during the excavation of the Culver Well site at Portland: when some of the limestone paving was removed it was found to be covering a stone-lined cavity in which had been placed a perforated scallop shell, a tranchet axe and a large round Chesil Beach pebble. There is no functional explanation for this.

One of the most famous mesolithic finds from Britain is the perforated stag-antler frontlets from Star Carr. These had been worked around the edge of the skull and were presumably intended to be worn on the head. There is one near-complete example, three other broken ones and several fragments. Figure 33 shows a complete example found on an early mesolithic site at Bedburg in the Rhine valley of Germany. This shows that the making of these perforated stag-antler frontlets was a mesolithic practice and not restricted to Star Carr. It has been suggested that they were worn on the head during a deer hunt to allow the hunter to approach the animals without them realising it. An alternative suggestion is that they were worn by shamans during ceremonial deer dances.

6
Separated by the sea

It was in the seventh millennium bc that Britain became an
island, probably around 6500 bc. As previously stated, this is
used as a convenient division between the earlier and later
mesolithic periods. It would seem that contacts with the Low
Countries or northern France gradually ceased and a more
insular mesolithic developed. Nearly three thousand years were
to pass before food-producing economies were to oust the
traditional hunting and foraging. This is almost twice as long as
the duration of the early mesolithic, a time as long as from the
bronze age to the present day. Yet less is known in many
respects of these later mesolithic groups than of their ancestors,
mainly because few well preserved sites with organic remains
have been discovered or excavated. For the most part, the
known sites are surface concentrations of flints. There is some
evidence for possible dwelling structures, dated hearths and a
few other features as described in the previous two chapters, but
only in some of the excavated coastal middens have any of the
more perishable, organic remains been recovered.

It is an enormously long period and some developments can
be discerned. Archaeologically, the only major change in the
flintwork was the introduction of many different forms of microliths with distinctive geometric shapes, often of very small size.
It has been suggested that they were purposely made to be
distinctive, with different hunting groups using their own particular types so that they would recognise each other's. This could
have been important for territorial or social reasons. The spread
of dense deciduous forest may have reduced the area suitable
for hunting and as a result a more rigid regard for some of the
traditional boundaries would have been required, especially in
areas that could still be kept clear by controlled firing. There
also seems to have been an increase in the exploitation of
marine resources from the Scottish islands to the south-western
coast of England. Otherwise, later mesolithic groups continued
to enjoy their traditional lifestyle.

While they did so, great changes were taking place across the
sea in Europe as, in the fifth millennium bc, people were
spreading westwards along the Danube, introducing a sedentary
life based on agriculture and pastoral farming. The indigenous
mesolithic population reacted in various ways: abandoning

their own way of life rapidly and adopting the new one, or making a compromise and adopting it only partially. The Ertebolle Culture of Denmark is a perfect example of the latter: the people still fished and hunted but copied the idea of making pottery and grinding their stone axes; and impressions of cereal grains in their pottery and some wooden spades indicate that they raised a few crops. They also kept a few domesticated sheep and cattle.

Nothing like this happened in Britain, even on the east side where some contact might have been expected. On the west side of Britain, a maritime economy may have developed, for it appears that there was contact across the water from Ireland to the Isle of Man, and between the Scottish islands. This was probably a direct result of groups of specialised marine fishermen who had mastered the construction of seaworthy craft. It has been suggested that by the fourth millennium bc a fraternity of fishing groups exploited the Atlantic seaboard from Scotland to Brittany. From the latter region they may have brought back ideas that were transforming the populations there, such as the building of megalithic tombs and, ultimately, other neolithic innovations. It seems to be more than a coincidence that the earliest known megalithic monuments follow the pattern of this mesolithic coastal distribution. Radiocarbon dates of the tombs at Carrowmore, County Sligo, are as early as 3800 ± 85 bc and a hearth on a neolithic site at Ballynagilly, County Tyrone, is 3795 ± 90 bc.

34. Microliths of later mesolithic date. (Top) White Gill, North Yorkshire. (Bottom left) Farnham, Surrey. (Bottom right) High Rocks, East Sussex. There was a tendency for geometric forms, often very diminutive. The larger hollow-based points are known as 'Horsham points' and are characteristic of sites in the Weald of south-east England. All actual size.

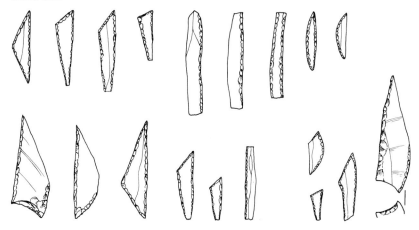

35. Footprints of a mesolithic beachcomber preserved in mud beneath peat at Uskmouth, Gwent, 'in the Severn estuary. (Photograph: D. Upton.)

What happened elsewhere is difficult to know, but by about the middle to end of the fourth millennium bc neolithic farming communities had been established in many parts of Britain. A few mesolithic radiocarbon dates do suggest an overlap, such as one from the Oronsay middens as recent as 3065 ± 210 bc. The date of a late mesolithic site in the Kennet valley near Hungerford, Berkshire, has a date of 3310 ± 130 bc, and it is only 14 km from the neolithic long barrow at Lambourn, Berkshire, which has a radiocarbon date of 3415 ± 180 bc. No mesolithic sites in Britain have been dated to the third millennium bc.

At present, only a guess can be made as to what happened. In the past it was generally considered that large numbers of settlers arrived with their domesticated animals, stores of seed grain and general equipment — pioneers in a new land that had a sparse native population which was no threat to them. The original inhabitants were either absorbed into the new society or, as 'second-rate citizens', gradually died out. However, there are significant differences between the types of monuments and pottery styles of the British neolithic and those of elsewhere in Europe. It thus seems more likely that the numbers of new settlers were minimal and that the existing mesolithic population, impressed with the idea of food production, soon obtained enough grain and livestock to adopt the system. The clearance of land by fire and axe was nothing new to them. Within a few generations the lifestyle of the mesolithic hunter-gatherers could have been forgotten.

7
Museums

Apart from the shell mounds of the Scottish Obanian sites, the mesolithic period has left no visible monuments on the landscape. The only excavated site preserved for display is the Abinger 'pit dwelling' listed below. However, most museums have some local mesolithic material (usually flintwork) on display. Those listed below are of particular interest in this respect.

Abinger Mesolithic Site and Museum, Abinger Manor, Abinger, Dorking, Surrey. Visits by prior arrangement with Mr or Mrs R. S. Clarke. Telephone: 0306 730760.
Ashmolean Museum of Art and Archaeology, Beaumont Street, Oxford OX1 2LM. Telephone: 0865 278000.
Bolton Museum and Art Gallery, Le Mans Crescent, Bolton, Lancashire BL1 1SE. Telephone: 0204 22311 extension 2191.
Brighton Art Gallery and Museum, Church Street, Brighton, East Sussex BN1 1UE. Telephone: 0273 603005.
Cambridge University Museum of Archaeology and Anthropology, Downing Street, Cambridge CB2 3DZ. Telephone: 0223 333516 or 337733. Finds from Star Carr.
Castle Museum, Norwich, Norfolk NR1 3JU. Telephone: 0603 222222 extension 71224. Leman and Ower barbed point.
Cheddar Show Caves Exhibition and Museum, Cheddar Gorge, Cheddar, Somerset BS27 3QF. Telephone: 0934 742343. Skeleton of 'Cheddar Man'.

City of Bristol Museum and Art Gallery, Queens Road, Bristol, Avon BS8 1RL. Telephone: 0272 222000.

Cornwall County Museum (Royal Institution of Cornwall), 25 River Street, Truro, Cornwall TR1 2SJ. Telephone: 0872 72205.

Farnham Museum, Willmer House, 38 West Street, Farnham, Surrey GU9 7DX. Telephone: 0252 715094.

Guildford Museum, Castle Arch, Quarry Street, Guildford, Surrey GU1 3SX. Telephone: 0483 444750.

Horsham Museum, Causeway House, 9 The Causeway, Horsham, West Sussex RH12 1HE. Telephone: 0403 54959. Finds from rich local sites on the greensand.

Hunterian Museum, University of Glasgow, Glasgow G12 8QQ. Telephone: 041-330 4221. Finds from Scottish coastal sites.

The Manchester Museum, University of Manchester, Oxford Road, Manchester M13 9PL. Telephone: 061-275 2634.

Museum of London, London Wall, London EC2Y 5HN. Telephone: 071-600 3699. Finds from the Thames.

National Museum of Wales, Cathays Park, Cardiff, South Glamorgan CF1 3NP. Telephone: 0222 397951. General display from Welsh mesolithic sites.

Newbury District Museum, The Wharf, Newbury, Berkshire RG14 5AS. Telephone: 0635 30511. Finds from the Kennet valley.

Pitt Rivers Museum, Parks Road, Oxford OX1 3PP. Telephone: 0865 270927. In the Department of Ethnology and Prehistory at 60 Banbury Road there is no display of British mesolithic material but it is the only museum in Britain with an anthropological display devoted to the life of pre-agricultural people from the most ancient time to the present, with much that is relevant to the mesolithic period.

Royal Museum of Scotland, Chambers Street, Edinburgh EH1 1JF. Telephone: 031-225 7534.

Sheffield City Museum, Weston Park, Sheffield, South Yorkshire S10 2TP. Telephone: 0742 768588.

Tunbridge Wells Museum and Art Gallery, Civic Centre, Mount Pleasant, Tunbridge Wells, Kent TN1 1RS. Telephone: 0892 26121 extension 3171. Finds from High Rocks.

Yorkshire Museum, Museum Gardens, York, North Yorkshire YO1 2DR. Telephone: 0904 629745. Finds from the Wolds and Moors.

8
Further reading

General

Bonsall, C. (editor). *The Mesolithic in Europe.* John Donald, 1989. A large, lavishly illustrated volume with papers on every aspect of the mesolithic period.

Clark, J. G. D. *Mesolithic Prelude: the Palaeolithic-Neolithic Transition in Old World Prehistory.* Edinburgh University Press, 1980.

Jacobi, R. M. 'Britain inside and outside Mesolithic Europe', *Proceedings of the Prehistoric Society,* 42 (1976) 67-84.

Mellars, P. (editor). *The Early Postglacial Settlement of Northern Europe.* Duckworth, 1978.

Rowley-Conwy, P.; Zvelebil, M.; and Blankholm, H. P. (editors). *Mesolithic Northwest Europe: Recent Trends.* Department of Archaeology and Prehistory, University of Sheffield, 1987.

National surveys

Morrison, A. *Early Man in Britain and Ireland.* Croom Helm, 1980. The only authoritative general account of the mesolithic period in Britain, with full references to sources.

Palmer, S. L. *Mesolithic Cultures of Britain.* Dolphin Press, 1977. Details of many sites, but restricted to southern England.

Woodman, P. C. *The Mesolithic in Ireland.* British Archaeological Reports, 58 (1978).

Wymer, J. J. (editor). *Gazetteer of Mesolithic Sites in England and Wales with a Gazetteer of Upper Palaeolithic Sites in England and Wales* (edited by C. J. Bonsall). Research Report of the Council for British Archaeology, 20 (1977).

Regional and county surveys

Barringer, C. (editor). *Aspects of East Anglian Pre-history.* Cambridge University Press, 1984.

Berridge, P., and Roberts, A. 'The Mesolithic Period in Cornwall' in R. Whimster and D. Harris (editors), Silver Jubilee volume, 1961-86, of *Cornish Archaeology,* 25 (1987).

Bird, J., and Bird, D. G. *The Archaeology of Surrey to 1540.* Surrey Archaeological Society, Guildford, 1987.

Buckley, D. G. *Archaeology in Essex to AD 1500.* Research Report of the Council for British Archaeology, 34 (1980).

Case, H. *The Mesolithic and Neolithic in the Oxford Region.* Oxford University Department of Extra Mural Studies, 1986.

Drewett, P. L. (editor). *Archaeology in Sussex to AD 1500.* Research Report of the Council for British Archaeology, 29 (1978).

Leach, P. E. (editor). *Archaeology in Kent to·AD 1500.* Research Report of the Council for British Archaeology, 48 (1982).

Shennan, S. J., and Schadla Hall, R. T. (editors). *The Archaeology of Hampshire: from the Palaeolithic to the Industrial Revolution.* Monograph of the Hampshire Field Club and Archaeological Society, number 1 (1981).

Some major site reports
Clark, J. G. D. *Excavations at Star Carr.* Cambridge University Press, second edition with new preface, 1971.

Mellars, P. *Oronsay: Prehistoric Human Ecology on a Small Island.* Edinburgh University Press, 1987.

Rankine, W. F. 'A Mesolithic Chipping Floor at the Warren, Oakhanger, Selborne, Hampshire', *Proceedings of the Prehistoric Society*, 18 (1952).

Wymer, J. J. and Churchill, D. M. 'Excavations at the Maglemosian sites at Thatcham, Berkshire, England', *Proceedings of the Prehistoric Society*, 28 (1962).

Local guides
Bramwell, D. *Archaeology in the Peak District.* Moorland Publishing, 1973.

Palmer, S. L. *Foodgatherers of Portland.* In press.

Index

Page numbers in italic refer to illustrations.

Mesolithic Britain